PRESENTED TO:

_____

FROM:

_____

DATE:

_____

WHAT WE WANT TO SAY TO GRADS

BARRY LANDIS
GENERAL EDITOR

David C Cook®
transforming lives together

WHAT WE WANT TO SAY TO GRADS
Published by David C. Cook
4050 Lee Vance View
Colorado Springs, CO 80918 U.S.A.

David C. Cook Distribution Canada
55 Woodslee Avenue, Paris, Ontario, Canada N3L 3E5

David C. Cook U.K., Kingsway Communications
Eastbourne, East Sussex BN23 6NT, England

The Web site addresses recommended throughout this book are offered as a
resource to you. These Web sites are not intended in any way to be or imply an
endorsement on the part of David C. Cook, nor do we vouch for their content.

ISBN 978-1-4347-6791-2

Published in association with the literary agency of Alive Communications, Inc.,
7680 Goddard St., Suite 200, Colorado Springs, CO 80920

The Team: Melanie Larson, Ingrid Beck, Amy Kiechlin, and Jaci Schneider
Cover Design: Disciple Design

Printed in the United States of America
First Edition 2009

1 2 3 4 5 6 7 8 9 10

020309

READ THIS ... PLEASE!

Okay, I know you are thinking that this is going to be another dry note from a publisher. That I'm going to say that the content of this book is very important and will shape your destiny and blah, blah, blah. The truth of the matter is that I have three sons—ages eighteen, nineteen, and twenty-one as I write this. Two of them are in college and one soon will be. I publish a lot of books, but this one hits close to home.

Obviously, I care about my sons' futures, which works out well because that means I care about your future, too. So it is with you in mind that this book came together. Us parents sometimes hate to admit it, but we know that a variety of people will play a significant role in your life, providing you with additional wisdom and insight you might not hear from us. So we wanted to gather a number of people who care about young people and ask them, "What would you want to communicate to someone starting out in life?" That's what this book is all about.

And check out the letter from Barry Landis on page 6 that explains how this book will help students who are interested in being Christians in secular environments—like a keygrip on a Hollywood set, a sound engineer in a New York studio, a backup singer in Las Vegas, or a road manager for a touring group.

We hope that what you find inside these pages will assist you. And maybe make you ask some questions. Maybe have you ponder God's role in your life. And maybe you will even laugh a time or two.

Oh, and thanks for reading this.

DON PAPE,
Publisher

FOREWORD

Thank you for picking up this copy of *What We Want to Say to Grads*. Many people have contributed to this work, and they are all dedicated to the idea that Christians need to influence our media and culture as positive role models. This notion is not new and was inspired in many of us by the late Bob Briner, who wrote the book *Roaring Lambs*. In his memory we established a not-for-profit organization called The Briner Institute, which seeks to achieve its primary mission of cultural engagement and influence through educational activities.

The Briner Institute and its members seek to *educate* interested persons in how to …

> ***Advocate*** for the proliferation of successful, quality faith- and family-based content movements in movies, music, games, and media.

> ***Mentor*** developing promising artists, writers, and musicians to provide a tax benefit to the inventor and artist community—whereby equity in small amounts is contributed up front to the institute, so that the future

success of these properties, artists, and creations perpetuates the institute's capital and endowment needs.

Network with likeminded persons globally in order to engage in the policy and culture-shaping mediums of expression that form and influence our cultural belief systems.

Provide scholarship to college-age "roaring lambs" with tuition grants, helping them acquire the necessary educational and professional credentials, so that they will be equipped to enter various culture-shaping careers with influence and credibility.

A portion of the proceeds of this book are being donated from David C. Cook to The Briner Institute, and we thank you for your help. To learn more about The Briner Institute, visit us at www.TheBrinerInstitute.org.

BARRY LANDIS
CEO of Landis Entertainment & Media Partners;
Executive Director of The Briner Institute

HARRY JACOBSON
Vice Chancellor for Health Affairs at
Vanderbilt University;
Chairman of the Board of The Briner Institute

CHOOSING YOUR FRIENDS

My son, Matt, is graduating in the class of 2009, and about a year ago he said something that stuck with me. He said that he had decided to choose friends based on who would help him to be who he really wants to be.

Now this is really smart, because most of us tend to "fall in" with people we happen to know or feel comfortable with, without ever being intentional about who we want to develop friendships with. But as you head into college or into the new world of life and work after college, you have the chance to break free from past connections and build new ones. And this time you can look around and purposely choose the people you want to build friendships with. You can target the people who know how to have fun but also make good choices. You can pursue friendships with people who are perhaps a step ahead of you in walking with God and living out their faith in the

world so they can draw you in that direction. You can choose to connect with people who are discovering the joy of living life for something and Someone greater than themselves rather than those who live like the world revolves around them.

Who you are going to be has a lot to do with who you are in relationship with. Choose your friends well and then love them well. Good friends of great character put the smile into life.

NANCY GUTHRIE
Author of *Holding On to Hope*

Listen, my son, to your father's instruction and do not forsake your mother's teaching.

Proverbs 1:8

DREAM BIG AND WORK HARD

Throughout our childhood our parents always stressed the importance of having a strong educational background. We are very fortunate to have found balance between our education and music career over the years, and we are still learning every day. We wish all graduates the best of luck as they experience this next chapter of their lives. Work hard and always dream big.

KEVIN, JOE, AND NICK
JONAS
The Jonas Brothers

MAKING LIFELONG FRIENDSHIPS

In 1985, I started a Bible study with three other guys from my dorm at the University of North Carolina. We prayed for each other, played ball together, studied God's Word together, and eventually shared an apartment. We became best friends. During our senior year, in 1988, we went on spring break together. Each one of us took about two hours to share our hopes, dreams, and concerns for life after graduation. We then prayed for each person. At the end of that spring break, we committed to get together every year for the rest of our lives.

And we've done it ever since. None of us makes a major decision in life without asking for input from the other three. We continue to share our hopes, dreams, fears, and frustrations. We've been there for each other to celebrate marriages and children. We've been there for each other through some extremely difficult times. I don't think I would be anywhere close to the man God wants me to be without David, Dave, and Tom.

As you graduate, I encourage you to commit to lifelong friends. You will make new friends along the way, but if you have a group of Christian friends already, it will be tough to replace that history. Make sure they know all about you now—be brutally honest—so that twenty years from now you have people who will call your bluff and love you anyway. God puts people into your life to mold you into His image.

KEVIN FORD
Chief Visionary Officer,
Managing Partner of
The Armstrong Group

TRUST GOD WITH YOUR FUTURE

Don't feel like you need to have your entire future planned out in advance. For lack of a better idea, I went to mortuary college after I graduated. I wanted to be a pathologist but couldn't afford medical school, so I thought being a mortician would be the next best thing. I expected to be embalming really old people who died of natural causes, but I embalmed so many who died in their twenties or thirties because of AIDS or suicide following an HIV-positive diagnosis. With my promiscuous past, I often thought, *It's only by God's grace that I'm standing over this embalming table rather than lying on top of it.*

God used those experiences to awaken a passion in me to help other young people avoid a similar fate. I began speaking publicly about the dangers of premarital sex, and eventually sensed God leading me to Teen Mania Ministries, where I began writing, teaching, and counseling women who'd looked

for love in all the wrong places as I once had. This passion for sexual purity became a fire in my bones, so when asked to write the Every Woman's Battle series, I only had to fast and pray about that for three seconds. I knew this was exactly what I was made to do.

If you're wondering what you were made to do, don't stress about figuring it all out today. As Psalm 37:4 says, "Delight yourself in the LORD, and he will give you the desires of your heart." Even if you don't know what those desires are yet, simply listen for His voice and obey one step at a time. Someday you'll look back in amazement at how God has ushered you down a path so wonderful that you could've never created such a life for yourself.

SHANNON ETHRIDGE, MA
Best-selling Author and Advocate for
Sexual Integrity, Sexual Intimacy, and
Intimacy with Christ

BEHOLD

It's easy to look. It's easy to glance, notice, brush past, then forget. But beholding is difficult. Beholding means time, and effort, and commitment. Beholding means putting your life on hold for a while and recharging your soul by marveling at the only thing capable of satisfying it. It means stopping what you're doing and staring in wonder—at creation, at people, and ultimately at the God who made them. You can glance at a TV show, or a commercial, but you wouldn't glance at the Grand Canyon. So don't glance at God. Instead, behold.

Go outside at night and behold. That line of three stars, Orion's belt, has a flaming purple seahorse behind it; that light left its origin when the Romans were still ruling Europe. "Is not God high in the heavens? See the highest stars, how lofty they are!" (Job 22:12 ESV).

Drink water and behold. There are more water molecules in half a pint than there are blades of grass on the entire earth. Who made them, and what keeps them in place? "He is before all things, and in him all things hold together" (Col. 1:17 ESV).

Climb mountains and behold. Man's achievements—algebra, postmodernism, Las Vegas—look a fair bit smaller from the top of Mount McKinley, and God's creation—clouds, the human eye, the sun—look a fair bit bigger. "Get you up to a high mountain, O Zion … say to the cities of Judah, 'Behold your God!'" (Isa. 40:9 ESV).

God appears on mountains rather than in malls, in windstorms rather than in superstores. And He does that for a reason. He doesn't want us to glance at Him for amusement, but to gaze at Him in amazement. He wants us to behold.

ANDREW WILSON
Author of *Incomparable* and
GodStories

This is what the Lord says— "… I am the Lord your God, who teaches you what is best for you, who directs you in the way you should go."

Isaiah 48:17

CHOOSE GOD'S PLAN

One lesson I learned after graduating was that making plans for yourself—both short- and long-term plans—is a good idea. But beware. Don't get so caught up in following your plans that you miss the direction the Lord is taking you.

Had I followed my own five-year plan I would quite possibly have a physical therapy practice somewhere in Canada. Instead, because I was willing to take a risk and let go of my own plan, I have been able to travel as a professional musician and be a part of what God is doing around the world—a career path I never even dreamed of pursuing.

This Bible passage rings true in my life: "'For I know the plans I have for you,' declares the Lord, 'plans … to give you hope and a future'" (Jer. 29:11). My life experiences have been so much richer because I chose His plan, not mine.

JEREMY THIESSEN
Drummer for *downhere*

VISION GUARANTEES SUCCESS

Let God's vision be your own. One of my favorite scriptures in the Bible is Proverbs 29:18 (ASV): "Where there is no vision, the people cast off restraint." Vision will keep you sharp and alert even in difficult situations. It will also help you find the hidden opportunities that no one else sees. Many times, the professional world can be wrought with complicated circumstances and negative people. With a unique vision from God, you are able to find hidden blessings and see the good in unpleasant situations.

In the parable of the talents in the New Testament, the workers were praised for being faithful with the talents they were given. Two people can be given the same opportunities and abilities, but their lives can yield different results. Without vision, you might not even recognize the chances for success that God has placed in front of you. The person with diligence, perseverance, and the vision of God can rise to the challenges set before him or her. The person who complains and finds fault with everything and everyone will most likely be empty-handed at the end of the day. A complainer is also usually jealous of other people's long-awaited victories.

So ignore the mediocrity and the naysayers you may encounter! Keep your vision and invest your talents. Don't be discouraged if you have to wait for the fullness of God's vision in your life to come to pass. The promise of Proverbs 22:29 is that a skilled man or woman will "serve before kings; he will not serve before obscure men."

JEN WATERS
Journalist and Songwriter

ENJOY THE RIDE

Walt Disney World, where I started my career and which provided some of my earliest childhood memories, serves as a perfect metaphor for life. Ever since I visited the Magic Kingdom as a little girl and rode my first roller coaster, I have been captivated by the thought that our lives are really one raucous, never-ending Space Mountain. Life is a wild ride full of thrills and adventures, twists and turns, ups and downs. New sights, fresh sounds, and unforeseen experiences come at us with amazing speed.

One moment we are slowly climbing an incline, our adrenaline pumping. We can't imagine feeling any better. Suddenly, we scream downhill so fast we think we might die. We are thrown in sudden turns—right, then left, then upside down. Sometimes we feel nauseous but we fight it, refusing to admit defeat. We are tempted to get off the ride if only we knew how.

But we find inner strength and push ahead. For me, God is my inner strength, "the stronghold of my life" (Ps. 27:1).

My advice to you: Anchor your life in Christ. Let Him be your stronghold through all of life's thrills and spills. If you let Him, God will be your lap bar, the One who keeps you from flying off the rails. Whether you are up or down—and, believe me, you will be both—He will always be with you. Have a great ride: Grab hold of Jesus and don't let go.

JODY DREYER
Senior VP of Marketing,
The Walt Disney Studios

A righteous man is cautious
in friendship, but the way
of the wicked leads them astray.

Proverbs 12:26

FRIENDS AFFECT YOUR FUTURE

In high school an old man told me something that I have never forgotten. He said, "Show me your friends and I will show you your future." I carry this thought around with me, even to this day.

So I say to you: choose your friends wisely, for they will shape your thoughts, habits, values—and the way you view the world—more than you could ever realize at this very moment.

J. R. BRIGGS
Author of *When God Says Jump*

DISCOVER WHO YOU ARE

I like the story of the poet who, when asked when he became such, answered, "We're born poets. We're born with an impulse to name the world. The question is not: When did I become a poet? The question is: When did you stop being one?"

The most pressing question facing you right now, or so it seems, is What will I become? You're asking it. Your parents, uncles, teachers, pastor, siblings, and friends are all asking it. What will you make of your education, your strengths, and your opportunities? What's next? Maybe you received a scholarship and need to choose a place and a course of study. Maybe a job prospect looms, travel beckons, or the idea of doing nothing for a while lures you. But arched over all these things is a constant wondering, *What will I become? Will I become a pilot? a carpenter? an artist? a dentist?*

The question is an important one. But so is this: What should you remain?

The prodigal son obsessed over the question of becoming. He felt stifled in his father's house. Life fell into safe, dull, predictable patterns. No surprises. No thrills. No adventures. He felt stuck in the dreary sameness of it all. So he left. To find himself. To make something of himself. To become someone.

Well, you know the story: It didn't go well. And here's why, I think: His mistake wasn't his leaving, or his seeking, or his wanting to become something. His mistake was that he wanted these things so desperately, he completely forgot who he already was: a son. The one the father loved, welcomed, and lavished his best upon.

Become what you will. We all want that for you. But never forget who you are. You are a child of the Father—deeply loved, always welcome. Always.

MARK BUCHANAN
Pastor and Author of *Your God Is Too Safe*

TAKE CONTROL OF YOUR MONEY

Very shortly, if not already, you will find yourself making more money then you ever have before. You could be rolling in the dough, but don't celebrate too soon—even folks with the best-paying gigs still find themselves broke!

So, what do you do with your paycheck? Do you know where your money's going? Consider it a silent partner in the successful business of You, Inc. If you don't already have a plan, let me give you a few ideas to get started.

Have a budget. Plan out on paper, on purpose, how you will give, save, and spend every dollar before the month begins. That way you'll take control of your money before it takes control of you!

Have an emergency fund! Bad things happen, but you can plan for them. Specifically, set aside $500–$1000 for that unexpected event.

Don't go into debt! Don't buy stuff with money you don't have just to impress people you don't even like. If you can't afford to pay cash, then you can't afford it. If you have debt, pay it off. If you are using your money to pay someone else, then you're not paying yourself. Your biggest wealth-building tool is your income.

Pay with cash. Our grandparents used the envelope system to help keep their spending where it should be. For example, if you eat out a lot, budget that money and put it in an envelope labeled "Restaurant." When you're out of cash … it's time to eat at home!

GIVE! Money's great! But don't be a jerk who just happens to have a lot of money. To whom much is given much is expected. Bless others because you have been blessed. It's not how much you have that counts, it is what you do with what you have that matters!

Become a generation of change! Live like no one else so later you can LIVE like no one else!

DAVE RAMSEY
Best-selling Author and
Nationally Syndicated Radio Talk
Show Host of *The Dave Ramsey
Show*

THE ART OF BEING TEACHABLE

One of the clearest memories from my time in graduate school was the day when a test we had taken was given back to us. The professor, a highly renowned man in his field of study who had years of educational and real-world experience, was explaining to one of the students why the answer he chose was not correct. Instantly, the student was up in arms, defending his position with absolutely no respect for the professor or his vast knowledge. I am not saying that professors are always correct, but this story shows how far we have come from being teachable and willing to be corrected.

Hebrews 12:11 says, "No discipline seems pleasant at the time, but painful. Later on, however, it produces a harvest of righteousness and peace for those who have been trained by it." And 1 Peter 5:5–6 reads, "Young men, in the same way be submissive to those who are older. All of you, clothe yourselves

with humility toward one another, because, 'God opposes the proud, but gives grace to the humble.' Humble yourselves, therefore, under God's mighty hand, that he may lift you up in due time."

You have just completed a major life phase and are graduating—congratulations! But no matter what phase of life we are in, we will never be perfect or all knowing. Let's humble ourselves so that God can teach us, correct us, and encourage us, even if through the mouths of our parents, teachers, professors, or bosses. This truth, like all those found in Scripture, holds true whether you are a student for life or a professional musician touring the world.

ERIC PATRICK
Flyleaf Road Pastor

Get wisdom, get understanding;
do not forget my words or
swerve from them.

Proverbs 4:4–6

THE ART OF BEING TEACHABLE
PART 2

The Bible says that in the last days people will not listen to sound doctrine and they will be lovers of themselves. They will gather around teachers who say only what their ears are itching to hear. I want to say amen to Eric's words because he has seen me with a "live by my feelings and only hear what I want to hear" heart. Thankfully, my heavenly Father would never let me stay that way.

I would not have matured past that point if God had not let me reap the destruction that came from sowing my own arrogance. You don't have to learn that way! You don't have to regret wasting your time only to learn later that you should have gotten wisdom by fearing God and heeding warnings. Humble yourself and listen to godly people who speak about the hard issues so that you can avoid them.

LACEY STURM, FLYLEAF
Lead Vocalist

BURNED OUT?

Perhaps that phrase perfectly described you, racing to finish your last set of finals and the end of your semester. We wonder, though: Could the phrase "burned out" ever describe your faith?

At different points, we've felt worn out and used up: by the church, by Christians, by religion. We knew—at least intellectually—that the Lord didn't place heavy weights of perfectionism or legalism on us. God's Word declares, "His commandments are not burdensome" (1 John 5:3 NASB).

Here's the trouble: The life of faith often feels difficult—almost impossible. Nonbelievers claim that religion is "all about do's and don'ts; it's just another set of rules." Even though Christians aren't supposed to agree, we sometimes secretly struggle with the same objections. Is obeying God like crossing a tightrope?

Are we doomed to a life of "never good enoughness"?

Absolutely not! Christ hasn't given us a tightrope to follow, but a compass and a guidebook. God offers you a map for healthy and holy living: the Bible. He also promises to dwell within you—to act as your compass. Listening to the Holy Spirit helps you consistently recalibrate your life, according to His ways.

Living a tightrope faith will exhaust you. That's why Jesus said, "Are you tired? Worn out? Burned out on religion? Come to me. Get away with me and you'll recover your life. I'll show you how to take a real rest. Walk with me and work with me—watch how I do it. Learn the unforced rhythms of grace. I won't lay anything heavy or ill-fitting on you. Keep company with me and you'll learn to live freely and lightly" (Matt. 11:28–30 MSG).

JERAMY & JERUSHA CLARK
Best-selling Authors of *I Gave Dating a Chance*

DON'T BE IN SUCH A HURRY

When I graduated from high school, I couldn't wait to grow up.
I thought that meant getting married (by age twenty), having
children (by age twenty-one), getting a job, working hard, and
buying things. Don't get me wrong, I love my children and I
have no regrets.

But I wish I could go back and tell myself yesterday what I've
been telling my adult children today: Do what you can do while
you still can, before you have to do all the things you'll have to
do.

Here's what it's like. Between the ages of eighteen and twenty-
four, your college years—if you don't tie yourself down with
early constraints—you are a bird. The cage door has been left
wide open. The wind is calling your name. Go on a mission
trip. Travel. Taste new foods. Take a road trip. Meet people. Get

involved in your community. Serve somebody. Dream it. Try it.

You might get burned. In fact, I can almost guarantee that you'll get singed once or twice. But so what if your goose gets cooked? You're still young. Go find another goose. You'll learn some valuable lessons along the way and you'll have some great stories to tell your kids.

When that happens—marriage, kids, career—it will usher in a long season of "have to's." It's an important time of your life and the world needs what you have to offer. But you don't have to do it right this minute. Spread your wings first. Lose a few feathers. You can start building a nest tomorrow.

MARTY LONGE
Author of *Boomtown*

A BIT OF ADVICE

Don't spend all your money on pizza and late-night ice cream; it's a good way to gain the freshman fifty (yeah … I mean the freshman fifty). And just because the four for twenty dollars previewed DVD sale at Blockbuster is amazing doesn't mean you have to buy something every time it is offered. You will need that money for something else.

Begin reading Oswald Chambers's *My Utmost for His Highest.* It will be encouraging in those moments of doubt. Read the gospels and see where, who, how, and why Jesus interacts with who He interacts with … that study will change your life. Above all, remember that God will always love you and that we are all children of God.

Remember that God can be found in the big things but also in the small things. When there is good in the world God is there. Every act of kindness makes God smile.

You were created in the image of God … be comfortable in the skin that He has given you. And above all, love God and love others because in the end love will win out!

MATT WILSON
Campus Minister
Newark, Delaware

Even if someone lived a thousand
years—make it two thousand!—but
didn't enjoy anything, what's the point?

Ecclesiastes 6:6 MSG

MAKE FUN A WAY OF LIFE

Spend as much time with your friends and family as possible! You're about to leave what you know and venture on into a new part of life, so make your last few memories good ones. There have been so many times when I've felt too tired to go to a football game or to a movie with my friends, and sometimes I missed out on the best fun.

Have a good time with your friends. And don't forget your family! You will miss them a lot more than you think, so have more family dinners together; take a big road trip somewhere fun.

I keep repeating the word *fun*, but it's so important. Have fun. And don't forget that the end of school isn't the end of the world. There is so much more out there that you are about to experience, so get ready, but don't forget to really make this last year count.

CAMMIE HALL, AGE 17
The Rubyz

GIVE IT ALL TO GOD

First Peter 5:7 (NLT) says, "Give all your worries and cares to God, for he cares about you." Okay, cool! But how do we really do that?

Many of us can't even keep track of the times people have told us not to worry and to just "give it to God." Good advice, but what does this mean exactly? For most of us, we muster all our faith to believe that everything will work out in the end, but struggle with giving our problems to the Lord one day and taking them back the next. We're like a gardener who plants a seed and worryingly digs it up to see how the roots are growing, doing more damage than good. Does that sound like you?

I think we can all admit that we struggle with that line between what I should control and what the Lord controls. How much am I supposed to do or how little? And how do I build up my faith enough to consistently "give it to God" and not worry?

I would encourage you to grab a friend today and dig into God's amazing Word. By learning about His ways, you will no longer struggle on a day-to-day basis to muster the faith to "give it to God." It will just become natural for you. You'll gain an unwavering assurance that enables you to not only trust the Lord, but also trust that you will like where He's taking you.

My life motto: Challenges are what make life interesting; overcoming them is what makes life meaningful.

TAMMY TRENT
Acclaimed Singer, Songwriter, Author,
and Speaker

Everything that was written in the past was written to teach us, so that through endurance and the encouragement of the Scriptures we might have hope.

Romans 15:4

KEEP AN EYE ON THE REARVIEW

Keep an eye on life's rearview mirror every now and then. In life, as in driving, it helps to know where you've been. It's also good to see what's coming up from behind.

Being aware of the past also helps us know what worked, and what hasn't. That doesn't mean we should never retry something that failed. But be aware. Read history. And above all else, keep your Bible open.

Then if someone promotes change, you'll recognize what's fresh ... and what's recycled. Sometimes it takes a little homework to put it in perspective. But even after graduation, that kind of homework never really goes out of style.

ROBERT ELMER
Author of Books for Kids, Teens, and Adults
www.RobertElmerBooks.com

THE NEXT RIGHT THING

Upon graduation you will cross a major milestone and enter into a transitional stage of becoming an independent and responsible young adult. During this time it will be more important than ever that you transition from exploring and experiencing all of the things that you can do in your current stage of life and choose to do those things that are best for you. It will be a time of saying no or good-bye to some nice things or good things so that you can pursue the best things for your life.

The good news is that you don't have to worry about all of the years up ahead. You don't have to become overwhelmed with thousands of decisions that you will have to make in the future. You only have to do one thing every day and do it over and over

again. If you do this one thing you will find God's will for your life and you will experience a long life of purpose and meaning. So what is it that you have to do each and every day? It is this: Do the next right thing. It won't always be easy but it will always lead you to God's best for your life. You have the character and the courage to choose to do the next right thing no matter how difficult it may be.

STEVE ARTERBURN
Speaker, Radio Host, and Author of
the Best-selling Every Man's Battle
Series

DETECT YOUR PASSION

Here is what matters most: Tap into your passion. Your passion is a place where you belong, where you fit in, where you matter and what you do matters to you. It's where your desires can come to fruition—which means to bear fruit that will feed yourself and others.

If there's something you're interested in and it means something to you, run with it and see where it leads you. If fashion is your passion, for example, that doesn't mean you'll become a fashion writer or that you even want to become one. But if you recognize it as a thing that you love, your writing about fashion is more likely to flow freely, the experience of learning and conveying that knowledge to readers far more enjoyable.

Now for the difficult part. In our society, we have done everything possible to leave behind any complexity that the word *passion* demands. We speak of it in lingerie ads, adrenaline-junkie

excursions, and bad song lyrics by modern rock bands. But to my knowledge, only one recent product of our pop culture-crazed time—Mel Gibson's *The Passion of the Christ*—hints at that other meaning, the darker one. Do something you love, and you must suffer.

But if it's your passion, you'll keep doing it, through the hard times, through the suffering. Recognize what your heart beats for. Recognize what your passion is about. Figure out what it is you were born to do—and if you don't know, search for shreds of evidence with a private eye's zeal. It's not something you think about as much as something you feel. Leadership expert Steven Covey describes this in terms of "detecting rather than inventing" your life's mission.

That might not happen today, tomorrow, the next day, or the day after. It might change over time. But it's somewhere inside you waiting, like a wondrous story, to be discovered, reported, and written.

LOUIS R. CARLOZO
Entertainment Editor and Staff Writer
at the *Chicago Tribune*;
Mentor

DREAMS CAN CHANGE

Follow your dreams—but know that dreams can change. My lifelong dream was to become an author. My new dream job has a steady paycheck and benefits—including retirement. A girl can dream, can't she?

Here are a few tidbits of advice from my life:

Read.

Don't lie.

Laugh often. Weep, too. There is a time for both. Don't be embarrassed by either.

Travel.

Don't promise what you can't deliver.

Spend time with people over fifty and under five. They're cooler than you think.

Pray.

Savor good chocolate.

Don't be afraid to take risks.

Spend a day without technology—no cell phone, laptop, iPod, etc.—and just be still.

Floss.

Call your mother.

Send thank-you notes (for all those graduation gifts).

LAURA JENSEN WALKER
Award-winning Author of Numerous
Books, Including *Reconstructing
Natalie*, Women of Faith™ Novel of
the Year, 2006

WORDS OF WISDOM

I can think of a number of "best advice" moments I had as a
young man. Each one helped to shape me into the person I am
today. I got in a whole lot of trouble with my parents once and
spent some time in asylum at my grandparents'. My grandpa
didn't care to know what I did; he just told me, "Don't ever
do it again." In short, learn from your mistakes. To this day I
take apart my mistakes and try to learn from them. I grieve my
foolishness or lack of skill and then I move on to live another
day.

Which brings me to another great piece of advice: Live one day
at a time. Truthfully, that's all you can live. Living in the past or
the future is a waste of the present. And while you're doing all
that living in the moment, remember to "always confirm, never
assume." Once I made the mistake of driving all the way to
Santa Barbara from Sacramento for a gig that wasn't scheduled

until the following week. I was going off of a conversation I'd had with the club manager several weeks earlier. I assumed everything was as we had previously planned but it wasn't. Always confirm, never assume.

Some other outstanding advice I always come back to is this: You only get one chance to make a first impression. So take your time with things. Don't rush into stuff. Don't overthink it, but do some quality thinking about what you'll say, how you'll look, what you'll do. That's just smart. It's why people will tell you that poor planning leads to poor performance.

Finally, keep your hands clean. No one wants to shake a dirty hand as they welcome you into their office for a job interview. Oh, and say thank you, a lot.

CHARLIE PEACOCK
Author and Recording Artist

GOD WILL PREPARE YOU

Pay attention to where and how God may be at work in your life—He could be equipping you for a future giant.

Before God called David to slay Goliath, He gave him some lion and bear experience, and David remembered. David was a shepherd boy, working long hours, but not doing the things you would think necessary to prepare for a giant. When a lion and a bear confronted David, his responsibility was to protect his sheep, but he relied on God to bring down the animal.

Here's a point where it's easy go astray. Our preparation may not include traditional practice. David was prepared because he knew that God had delivered him from the lion and the bear. So when

Saul told the young shepherd boy that he didn't stand a chance against the giant who had been a soldier since youth, the boy answers, "The LORD who delivered me from the paw of the lion and the paw of the bear will deliver me from the hand of this Philistine" (1 Sam. 17:37).

Be aware of God's preparation, recognize His hand in delivering you from other threats, and you'll be ready to face the giant.

CHIP MURRAY
Managing Partner of The Panda Fund

As God's fellow workers we urge
you not to receive God's grace
in vain.... We put no stumbling block
in anyone's path, so that our
ministry will not be discredited.

2 Corinthians 6:1, 3

EMBRACE GRACE

Make grace the theme of your life. Be a picture of how wide and long and high and deep God's love is.

There are plenty of plank-eyed judges, record-keeping lovers, arrow-straight reflection worshippers, whitewashed fence-sitters, condescending radicals, truthful gossips, side-huggers, bitter forgivers, considerate bigots, cynical caregivers, empathetic loan sharks, coat-holding pacifists, zealous pearl-pawners, three-car treasure-buriers, serial petition-signers, rich young patronizers, and swivel-necked rule-keepers. The world doesn't need more of them.

You have been shown grace. Praise God and share it recklessly.

CHRISTOPHER GRANT
C. Grant and Company Marketing
Communications
Wheaton, IL

RECLAIM YOUR CULTURE FOR GOD

In the beginning of time we know that God created the heavens and the earth in His wisdom, His love, and with His genius imagination. He then created man in His image not only to worship Him but also to fill the earth, in which man would then build and govern a society. He gave man the insight and creativity to mold and shape our culture. But what once was evidence of God's honor and glory has now been duplicated, carbon-copied, and mass-produced so that we have forgotten where it came from. For centuries God and His church have inspired the greatest minds and the most influential musicians and artists of our time.

To this day God is searching for those of you willing to be used by His wisdom, love, and imagination to reclaim and restore our societies and cultures. In Him you have the knowledge, understanding, and God-given gifts to change this world back to

the way God first intended it to be. You have seen the past and now God has given you vision for the future. You are the hope of tomorrow and the heart, mind, and soul of a new revolution. You are the voice of today!

SONNY SANDOVAL, P.O.D.
Lead Vocalist

KEEP GROWING

In former generations a person set his or her career path in a linear fashion. It ideally moved undisturbed within one company or trade toward a gold watch retirement party. That sort of workplace rarely exists anymore. Our emergent work environments are fluid and evolve at lightning speed. It seems that one needs to reinvent oneself about every three to five years. Change is inevitable but growth is optional.

Therein lies your strategy. Keep growing. The entire experience of life can be used as a forum for learning. There is nothing that will happen to you from which you cannot learn! This process demands fearless honesty and the ability to constantly monitor your thoughts and feelings. Reflection on our thoughts, both instantaneously as they occur and later as a little time has passed, provides the opportunity to strategically analyze and change. We evolve!

A crucial element in this process is critique. Not the unconditional love that we get from loving family and friends, but the observations that come from those who are courageous enough to tell us what we need to hear. There are occasions when the most valuable information you will receive will come from someone who is unhappy, even furious with you. Dare to think that even someone who could be considered an "enemy" will provide you with knowledge about yourself that you can use. From your secure position of knowing that God and others love you, let the criticism come in just a little bit to see if there's something there that you can use for your own growth.

DAN KEEN
Vice President of ASCAP

Let us love one another, for love comes from God. Everyone who loves has been born of God and knows God. Whoever does not love does not know God, because God is love.

1 John 4:7–8

THE BEST YEARS OF YOUR LIFE

I remember the first time I tried surfing in Hawaii. I paddled out to where the waves were cresting and thought, *How hard can this be? I mean seriously, the IQ of surfers isn't exactly the highest in the world. This can't be that hard.* So I sat on the board anxiously awaiting my first wave. I was excited. I was scared. I was at peace. But I was a little fearful of the unknown.

The sun was just about to set, and I looked out over the horizon and felt the most overwhelming sensation of belonging. It was a surreal experience, almost spiritual, as I soaked in the bigness of a Creator who put everything into motion. I felt the worries of life fade away. It was just me and the ocean.

The sea started to swell. I glared at the ominous wave approaching and I could sense, this was the one. *I'm gonna dominate this!* I thought to myself. The wave rolled in and I

paddled like a madman. Suddenly I was standing on the board (for like three seconds), and then BAM! The next thing I knew I was tumbling at the bottom of the ocean. My eyes were stinging with salt, my ears were full of sand, and I felt my legs being cut on the coral below. I started to panic. *I'm gonna die!*

I finally found my way to the top of the water and saw my surfboard about thirty yards away. It was a great day of humiliation, but it was also a spiritual awakening for me. My ambition quickly fused into the reality of life, making my adventurous spirit take a backseat to the most important parts of the day.

In a similar way, you may be staring the next phase of your life in the face, thinking, *I'm gonna dominate this!* These are going to be some of the best years of your life. But if I could encourage you to do one thing well: Be sure you work on the development of your spirit.

Studies are essential, and friendships are key, but don't forget God created you as a spiritual being, and He can give you beauty in the midst of the waves.

Jesus said the two most important keys to life are: To "love the Lord your God with all your heart and with all your soul and with all your mind. This is the first and greatest commandment. And the second is like it: Love your neighbor as yourself" (Matt. 22:37–39). Your relationship with God will ground you in a sea of uncertainty, and your relationships with others will help develop the community God intended us to live in.

Rides will come and go, studies will stretch your mind; but the memorable parts of existence happen when we sit patiently and ponder God's wonderful beauty in the relationships He's laid before us. Now Go … Ride HARD!!

ANDY BRANER
President of Kanakuk Colorado

LIFE ISN'T FAIR

Some of us grew up in families where fairness was one of our primary family values. If you had a sibling, your childhood chores had to be split evenly; you may have shared dishwashing duty with your brother or sister, for example. But if you got stuck washing the dishes two days in a row, then boy, did you let everyone hear you complain.

We can look back at our childhood selves and laugh at such triviality, but the truth is, as graduating students, I bet that you still carry the mentality and expectation that life should give you a fair shake. And while the idea of fairness is a great value for each of us to cultivate and develop, the unfortunate fact is that this attitude is not transferable to life in general.

The sense that life is going to be fair, to give and take equally from each of us, is perhaps one of the unhealthiest of expectations.

Life is random. Life is full of chance. Life delivers its blessings unequally. Life's challenges, hurdles, and obstacles are often distributed unequally and, sometimes it seems, capriciously.

The net result of expecting life to be fair is that we begin to question why we were chosen for the horribly unfair treatment we are experiencing. We begin to believe some very unhealthy and unproductive notions. We begin to think like and act like victims. Being a victim robs us of our sense of freedom and it limits our ability to see the many possibilities that are available to us.

Of course, we should practice fairness with all of those we come into contact with in our lives. But to expect the same treatment in return is a setup for utter disappointment and disillusionment. Don't sit back, being a victim. Victims don't succeed and they don't win. Engage life, work to find your way, and never stop struggling to reach your dreams.

DEVLIN DONALDSON
Nontraditional and Relational
Marketing, Leadership Development
The Elevation Group

THIS IS YOUR LIFE

It is hard at the time of graduation to know what you want to do or strive to become, so my advice is to try lots of things until you find the right one for you. Don't be afraid to try something new or different. Keep exploring, experimenting, and following your passions.

During your journey try to surround yourself with mentors and other smart people whom you can learn from and emulate. You should try to build a reputation as a great listener, a team player, a quick learner, a hard worker, and a person who gets things done. If you can do these things you will be building the best "you."

Remember that it is okay to ask questions, be adventurous, and make mistakes. Failure can be a great teacher as long as you learn from it and try not to repeat the same mistakes.

Follow your instincts, inner voice, and judgment to recognize your ability to change your own behavior, environment, and experiences.

Lastly, be creative, determined, have a positive attitude, be polite, and remember to always have fun! This is your life—now go start living it your way and be the best you can be.

HOWARD S. BROWN
Cofounder and CEO of CircleBuilder.com
and PlanitJewish.com

LIVE TO LEARN

When I graduated from college the best advice I received was from a professor I admired. She told me to never stop learning. As simple as that might sound, it is the advice that I find myself passing on to my students now that I am the professor. Never stop learning.

You might feel that you have finished your education now that you are a graduate, but I encourage you to view your schooling as the foundation for all of the learning yet to take place in your life. You have laid a foundation for yourself and now you can build on it. In other words, the house still has not been built. That is what you do during the rest of your life. I encourage you to continue to read and expand your mind. Stay knowledgeable on the latest advances in your field. You should not only keep learning about your field, but you should also stay abreast of the events going on in the world around you.

Another piece of advice: Get involved in your community. It is vital that your voice is heard in your community and the world. The voices of young people in our communities are important, and your opinions matter. We need your new, innovative ideas to tackle the social issues facing us today. Do not hesitate because you are young. God used Josiah when he was just a child to bring honor back to his nation (2 Chron. 34—35). God can use you in the same manner to influence your world, community, industry, workplace, etc. He wants you to seek after Him and become an influential person to change your world.

JENIFER L. LEWIS, PHD
Carnegie Political
Engagement Scholar;
Assistant Professor of
Communication,
Western Kentucky University

Get along among yourselves, each
of you doing your part.... Gently
encourage the stragglers, and reach
out for the exhausted, pulling them
to their feet.

1 Thessalonians 5:13 MSG

WORK TO LIVE

Surround yourself with encouragers, not discouragers. Have an inner circle of advisers who are a mix of peers and those who are older and wiser. Ask for input from these trusted advisers before making any major life decisions, from buying a car to considering a job, to whom you should marry.

Do not take your talents and gifts for granted but seek to hone them and use them for the greater good. Tithe, pray, volunteer, serve others.

Finally, work to live, don't live to work.

RAY BLACKSTON
Author of *Flabbergasted*

BE A GOOD STEWARD

Now that you have graduated, you have reached a new place in your life journey. I believe that each of us is called for special purposes. Maybe it is a special job or a special relationship or a special service project or whatever. But whether you come at this subject from faith or not, we are all stewards of what has been given to us: this earth, our capabilities and resources, the community in which we live and work, and our professions.

Today more than ever our actions and decisions must consider the impact on the earth, its environs, its communities, and many people we do not know. Globally we are more connected today than ever before and that will only increase. We are dependent on each other, both in what we buy and consume, but also in what we make and how we process things … and of course the waste we produce.

I urge you to take up the mantle of efficient and responsible choices for the future. It will take the intelligence and passion of good stewards to both provide for our growing world and leave the environment in better shape than before. You are the beneficiaries of those who went before you, and now it is your turn to accept some responsibility for the future. You will determine how our quality of life will be shaped and how it will be passed on to the next generation.

I applaud your accomplishments and encourage you to think as a steward.

JOE C. COOK JR.
Principal and Cofounder of Mountain Group Capital;
Chairman of the Board of Directors of Amylin Pharmaceuticals, Inc.

May the Lord show you his favor
and give you his peace.

Numbers 6:26 NLT

PRAY FOR FAVOR

The greatest insight to discovering God's will for my life has been "finding favor." The biblical inspiration is found in the story of Joseph (Gen. 39:4). When I began to reflect on my life, I realized that my success or failure was almost always directly tied to someone else opening or closing a door for me. It became clear that the way others perceived me, often beyond my control, led directly to their taking action on my behalf.

Several years ago I began praying specifically for favor, that God would guide my path through the favor of others. My prayer is open-ended rather than specific, thus leaving everything to God's pleasure—not my attempt at manipulation. Finding favor requires faith, action through prayer, trust, and relinquishing control. Make note of your prayers and watch for ways that God works through the lives of others to guide your path.

JOHN MANNING HORTON
New Business Development Director,
Walt Disney Parks and Resorts

LIVE THE ADVENTURE

If there's one thing I've learned as a recent high school graduate, it's that we cannot live and dream within the confines of the world's box. My senior year I was buried under college applications and financial aid deadlines. Instead of experiencing the freedom of new opportunities, I felt more like I was caged in by the expectations that came along with them!

It wasn't until I realized the capacity of what was at my fingertips that I truly understood what was before me. God was calling me out of the comfortable, out of the normal, out of the apathetic compromise of "just getting by." This was my chance to be unleashed into an adventure that God called me to play an irreplaceable role in. Suddenly the world's pull and expectation seemed to fade. It was my duty in that crossroad not only to believe that I had gifts, but discover them … and *USE* them.

It is far too easy and common to succumb to sitting on the sidelines of life, simply because we cannot imagine God having a purpose for us. This is so heartbreaking to me, because not only does it strip us of personal value, but of dreams and motivation! First Corinthians 2:9 says, "No eye has seen, no ear has heard, no mind has conceived what God has prepared for those who love him." We serve a God who is not bound by the standard graduation course of the world. He has given us a life, a mist of time on this earth, to reach so much further than ourselves, and truly make a difference in the world.

So, at this beautiful crossroad in your life, I challenge you to play your irreplaceable role. Step outside of the world's box and use the life that you've been given.

PAIGE ARMSTRONG
Speaker for iShine Live Tour

REMEMBER THE THREE Ms

When the 3M Company created the sticky note, people were given the ability to leave short notes anywhere they wanted to remind themselves of things they didn't want to forget. No more paper clips, pins, tape, magnets, or staples. Here are three Ms that I hope will stick with you over the course of the next several years:

Marry Smart: You will marry only someone you have dated, so date smart. Date only those individuals who share the same passion you do for Christ and His calling. Nothing will have a greater impact on your ability and willingness to follow God's call on your life than your choice of a mate. Make sure that you agree on all the big things: faith, mission, kids, and money.

Money: Manage it or it will manage you. Next to your choice of a mate, the factor that will most impact your ability to follow God's

call on your life will be your ability, or inability, to handle money. Gain basic knowledge related to credit, debt, and budgeting—and the earlier the better. Learn how to use and balance your checking account. Use cash for just about everything.

Monitor the Monitor: Screens come in all shapes and sizes now, whether on cell phones, iPods, computers, televisions, DVD players, or Game Boys. With all of these gadgets comes a corresponding increase in screen time. Set limits on how much time each day you will spend in front of a screen. Manage your monitor time by adding other things to your life like face-to-face conversation, exercising, reading, hiking, going to plays, concerts, or museums. This will make you a well-rounded person who has the capacity and skill to deal with life and people.

Finally, it might be a good idea to write these three Ms on a sticky note and put them somewhere you will see them fairly often.

JON KULAGA
Provost of Asbury College

FALL BUT DON'T QUIT

If you don't fall down, you're not trying hard enough....

While studying dance at the University of Texas, I had an instructor who used to reiterate this phrase as we tried to do triple or quadruple turns with our bodies. Those who got bruises from the effort exerted ended up being the stars on stage. This same principle applies throughout life ... both professionally and personally.

While creating what is now the most popular radio entity for kids, my husband and I experienced several miscarriages. I was fit and under forty ... so God and I had some very heated discussions during that time; I couldn't understand why He kept letting me fall down. After I had three more failed attempts to become pregnant, He convinced me we were "turning" the wrong way. We finally heeded the advice of a friend who had encouraged us to contact an international adoption agency. Within one year our youngest daughter from Vietnam joined our family. Had I not fallen down because of my physical "limitations" or given up and not tried a different way, her glorious belly laugh and incredibly independent spirit would not be with us today.

Whatever you do, put your whole self into it. Jump in with every arm and leg you can find! When you fall down, move beyond the pain and feel grateful when you earn your bruises and scars; they will give you strength, knowledge, and character. Persevere, follow up with a new angle, and eventually you'll find success you never dreamed possible.

ROBIN JONES
VP of Business Development,
Starhaven and
Former VP of Programming for
Radio Disney

DREAM AND PLAN

When I was eighteen, I went to college but I also started a band. Which one was more important? At the time, I had no idea so I did both.

During the next four years of my life, I reached several forks in the road when I could have chosen one direction over the other. At one point I almost quit the band so I could focus on college. Another time, I almost dropped out of school because of the band. But at each juncture, I continued to pursue both. It wasn't until the band signed a recording contract and our touring schedule made attending school impossible that I chose the band.

My band is called Third Day, and we've done pretty well. We've sold some records and toured all over the world. We've even raked in a few awards and other accolades. By just about any standard, the band has been a success.

But I do not regret the time I spent in college. College equipped me with a writing ability that I have used to write songs, blogs, and magazine articles. The rigorous nature of school gave me a level of confidence to meet challenging deadlines. And I learned a whole lot about a lot of things.

If things had gone the other way, I am quite confident that I would be writing this same article, albeit from a slightly different perspective. I might be a college professor or lawyer or politician, and I would be looking back fondly at my years of being in a rock band and how that gave me a set of skills and experiences that I would not have otherwise.

Right now, you're standing on a precipice. Before you is a wide chasm filled with possibilities. It is exciting, but it can also be dizzying, even paralyzing. You probably have grand dreams as well as practical plans. My advice: Pursue both.

MARK LEE
Guitarist for Third Day

For Christ's love compels us ... that
those who live should no longer live
for themselves but for him who died
for them and was raised again.

2 Corinthians 5:14–15

IT'S NOT ABOUT YOU

Soon friends and family will begin offering their congratulations and praise for the things you have done and will do. Do not let yourself be fooled. Life is not about you. And it's not about me.

We are made not to live life for ourselves, but for others. Life is about the One who gave us Life, not about us. So go out and live as you were created to live.

MIKE & DANAE YANKOSKI
Authors and Speakers Engaging with
Social Justice Issues

CHOOSE YOUR FUTURE

"Seek first his kingdom and his righteousness and all these things will be given to you as well" (Matt. 6:33). This verse is an important promise to me. It implies that it is my choice to give my highest priority to following and obeying God.

The daily choices you make will determine your future. Make reading and studying God's Word a daily priority—even if it's only for a few minutes. The temptation may be to think that next month or next year there will be more time to pray and study the Bible. But now is the time to establish this important habit.

Seek God's will in determining a career and using the gifts and abilities He has given you. Each job is an opportunity to display integrity and diligence, thereby honoring God and showing Him to unbelieving and skeptical fellow workers.

Another critical choice is selecting true, godly friends who share

your values. These friendships will be a source of encouragement during difficult seasons and celebration in happy times. But be sure to develop acquaintances with unbelieving neighbors and friends. As you share your life with them, they will see Jesus in your responses to both good and adverse circumstances.

After choosing to follow God, the most important choice will be your husband or wife. Make this decision without haste and with much prayer. Discuss your dreams and goals thoroughly, making sure that you share the same interests and aims.

The future is before you. It is an unknown—frightening in many aspects but also hopeful and exciting. Live life expectantly and joyfully because God is your guide who loves and protects you. Cultivate an attitude of thankfulness, looking for the good in every situation.

"Above all else, guard your heart, for it is the wellspring of life" (Prov. 4:23).

MARTY BRINER
Wife of the Late Bob Briner

SOMETHING THAT CANNOT BE LOST

When I was much younger and just starting out in business, someone said to me, "Always tell the truth the first time and you'll never have to remember what you said." Those words hit me hard and became a lesson I've tried to take with me throughout my life.

James 5:12 (ESV) instructs us to "Let your 'yes' be yes and your 'no' be no, so that you may not fall under condemnation." And Mark Twain once said, "Always do right. This will gratify some people and astonish the rest."

Living your life in this manner leads to a life of integrity, and I believe that God is looking for people of integrity. Proverbs 10:9 (ESV) tells us that "Whoever walks in integrity walks securely, but he who makes his ways crooked will be found out." King David prayed in Psalm 25:21 (ESV), "May integrity and uprightness preserve me" and said again in Psalm 41:12 (ESV), "You have upheld me because of my integrity." Job, in the midst of all his testing, responded, "Let me be weighed in a just balance, and let God know my integrity!" (Job 31:6 ESV).

Integrity must be lived out every minute of every day. It is borne out in the difficult times, not just when we're looking our best or when everything is going our way. It is refined in crisis. It matters in our relationships and when we're alone.

The good news is that our integrity is one thing that cannot be taken from us … it can only be given away by our own choices and actions. May we daily choose to walk the path of integrity

NEAL JOSEPH
Senior VP of
International Partner Development,
Compassion International

NURTURE RELATIONSHIPS

In Hollywood, the most common advice for success is, "It's all about who you know." This is really a statement about developing relationships, and it is a crucial key to making your vocational dream a reality. The ability to genuinely be interested in people in your field and to actively work at nurturing relationships will make you stand out above the crowd. When people are looking for a person to fill a position, they will remember you.

At the beginning of your job search, connect with successful people in your field by offering to take them to coffee and asking about their experience or advice to a beginner. You will be surprised how many people wish to impart their wisdom to you.

During the interview process, building rapport with the employer is critical. Bring a list of good questions. It will show that you are sincerely interested in the way they do things. Questions may include: What are three things you value most in an employee? What is most frustrating? Where would you like your organization to be in three years? Also, listen carefully for a point of mutual interest to share briefly on a personal level. People want to work with someone they will enjoy and who is fun.

Once you are hired, foster relationships at every level. Offer a helping hand. Affirm others. Take initiative to create a better work environment. Build relationships with coworkers beyond work. Join professional organizations and work on their committees. Connect people. Instead of Christmas cards send Thanksgiving cards, expressing how thankful you are that these people are in your life.

Hollywood knows that building and nurturing relationship is the key to success, but it is also a goal congruent with a life of faith at its deepest level. This message is found in 1 Corinthians 13:4–5 (NIRV), "Love … does not look out for its own interests."

REBECCA VER STRATEN-MCSPARRAN
Director of L.A. Film Studies Center;
Founding Pastor of
Tribe of Los Angeles

"Risk your life and get more than you
ever dreamed of. Play it safe and
end up holding the bag."

Luke 19:26 MSG

RISK BEING UNCOMFORTABLE

Leave the borders of America, placing yourself in uncomfortable, difficult circumstances. Go to places that disturb you, that upset your idea of the American dream, so that you can dream kingdom-of-God dreams. Don't settle for complacent ordinariness. Dare to let God blow up your comfortable box. Dare to go places where only Jesus can pull you through.

Risk, resting in the sovereignty of God. And above all, strive to worship God wherever He leads you.

MARY E. DEMUTH
Speaker and Author of *Daisy Chain* and *Authentic Parenting in a Postmodern Culture*

Therefore, brethren, be even more
diligent to make your call and election
sure, for if you do these things you
will never stumble.

2 Peter 1:10 NKJV

WHAT SONG WILL YOU SING?

In the 2005 movie *Walk the Line*, the famous singer Johnny Cash and his band are trying to cut their first record. The producer stops them midsong and informs them that their work won't sell. To paraphrase, he asks them, "If you were hit by a truck and you could only sing one song before you died, what would that song be?" Cash then sings a song that he wrote from his heart, which became a smash hit and solidified his career.

So I ask you: If you could sing one song what would it be? What is your heart cry?

I believe God places a "heart cry" in each of us. It has been said that our calling is "that place where our deep delights meet the deep hungers of the world." Your calling and mission are how you want to be remembered. It is the song that you

have to sing. It is how you use your individual gifts, strengths, and abilities, in specific places, in specific ways, with specific people, for specific ends.

The Greek philosopher Plato told us that we should live a life that pursues beauty, truth, and goodness. I believe that was God-given insight. The busyness of life and the stresses you face can cause you to miss the joy of beauty, the power of truth, and the rewards of goodness. Regularly take a deep breath and feast your eyes on the beauty around you. Make every moment count. Observe the beauty of creation, the creativity of others, and the beauty and creativity that is found within you and wishes to express itself.

There are those who will tell you that there is no such thing as truth. Don't believe them. Pursue truth with all your heart and as Jesus said, it will set you free. There is no greater truth than Jesus Himself. God intends for us to ask questions and be filled with curiosity, to pursue wisdom and never stop learning.

An Asian proverb says, "Suffering is the one promise that life keeps." We all wander in the wilderness at times. We all suffer. The suffering of those around us can sometimes be absolutely overwhelming, leaving us feeling hopeless and helpless. But God does walk with us all the way. People who embrace fearlessness despite the difficulties of life have hope.

I believe the individual-oriented, self-focused culture we live in prevents us from understanding the power and significance of community. We are not intended to go it alone. Friends and family will help you understand your calling and mission. They will help you pursue goodness, truth, and beauty. They will encourage you to seek wisdom, continue learning, and remain curious. They will challenge you to never give up hope.

DR. RICHARD GATHRO
Assistant to the President,
Dean of Nyack College, Washington,
D.C.

Do good instead of evil and try to live
at peace. If you obey the LORD, he
will watch over you and answer
your prayers.

Psalm 34:14–15 CEV

BE GOOD

My dad would often say, "Be good to everyone because everyone is hurting." You often don't really know what people are going through. So be careful in your relationships. Having the ability to give people the benefit of the doubt (without being a pushover) is a great gift to cultivate. It saves you from the tyranny of being constantly offended. To be truly free to love others unselfishly frees God to use you and bless you in great ways.

"Let us not become weary in doing good, for at the proper time we will reap a harvest if we do not give up. Therefore, as we have opportunity, let us do good to all people, especially to those who belong to the family of believers" (Gal. 6:9–10).

SCOTT HARRIS
Missions Minister,
Brentwood Baptist Church

WHAT DO YOU VALUE?

Einstein once wrote, "Try not to become a man of success, but rather try to become a man of value." One of the important lessons in life is to make sure you define success for yourself or else your culture, peer group, or employer will define it for you.

Brandon Tartikoff, the legendary television executive, was a key mentor in my life. He once told me to determine the one job I most wanted to have and put myself on a path to get it. I thought that was wise advice but led to a narrow road because the job I envisioned only existed in a handful of places. What I learned, though, was that if I could come to grips with what I was good at and what suited my personality, the road to get there would be as fulfilling as the specific job itself.

I think God has uniquely gifted each of us. We also have distinct personality traits. If a person can discover his or her giftedness and be in the right environment for his or her personality, there are numerous occupations that will be satisfying. Being true to how you are wired is a key to being fulfilled in your work.

Ask yourself the tough questions. Work hard for that which you value. Don't let other people's values dictate what you should value. Spend your only irreplaceable commodity, your time, on that which you value. In the end the return on that investment is success.

TERRY BOTWICK
President of Vanguard Films and
Vanguard Animation

Love the Lord your God with all your heart and with all your soul and with all your mind and with all your strength.

Mark 12:30

DON'T FORGET TO THINK

Use your brain and use it often. Exercise your mind. Christians have a tendency to let other people tell them what they should think. We listen well because we've been trained to. It's what we do when we're in church on Sundays. But you must not let other people, be it a pastor or a parent, do your thinking for you. As Voltaire once said, "Think for yourselves and allow others the privilege to do so, too." You are responsible to God for the state of your soul. He has given you a mind with the intention that you will use it. So, what do *you* think? And why?

SIRI MITCHELL
Author of *Moon over Tokyo* and
Chateau of Echoes

HELPING HANDS

Open your hands and look at them. You will use these marvelous gifts for the honor and glory of God or you will use them for yourself. With them, you will serve God or you will serve money, but you cannot do both. Your hands will make idols you will worship, or they will create altars in praise of Him. By them, you will extend great kindness and comfort to others, even your enemies, or you will employ them in empty and destructive pursuits.

Open your hands and give thanks for them. Pray each day that the Father will place in your hands what He wants in them. Ask Him to remove from them anything that is not pleasing to Him. If you do this, you will be among a remarkably small percentage

of Christians willing to trust Him with every detail of their lives. You will discover what He chooses for you is always better than what you choose for yourself. Make this your daily prayer, and I assure you, it will be impossible to miss His will for your life or what He has designed you to accomplish. I dare you to join this joyful adventure of love.

WES YODER
President of Ambassador Speakers
Bureau & Literary Agency

SCRIPTURE REFERENCES

www.theBrinerInstitute.org